Flowers and Berries
in Cross Stitch

Pattern chart for design on front cover

ROSA VIRGINIANA

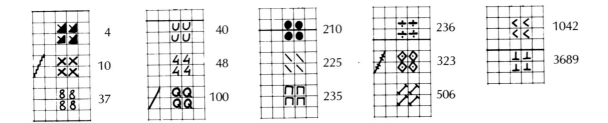

Flowers and Berries in Cross Stitch

With The Danish Handcraft Guild

Designed by Gerda Bengtsson

Bell & Hyman

Contents

Published in 1986 by
Bell & Hyman Limited
Denmark House
37-39 Queen Elizabeth Street
London
SE1 2QB

First published in Denmark by
Høst & Søns Forlag
Copenhagen in 1986
under the title:
Roser og blomstrende grene i korssting

© Selskabet til Haandarbejdets Fremme and
Høst & Søns Forlag
Copenhagen 1986

ISBN: 0 7135 2717 X

Typeset by August Filmsetting, St. Helens
Printed in Denmark.

Preface

Each year The Danish Handcraft Guild publishes a calendar of cross stitch designs. This book combines the flower designs from two such calendars.

The roses and berries in this book are designed by Gerda Bengtsson who is Denmark's most popular flower illustrator. She has worked extensively for the Danish Handcraft Guild and her reputation has spread to many parts of the world through her cross stitch designs.

Few people are as familiar with the Danish flora as Gerda Bengtsson. She is a flower connoisseur. When she observes flowers she always does so with a view to drawing them. She is aware that her roses and berries must not only be lifelike, but also have to be designed to make beautiful, artistic compositions.

In order to avoid large areas of single colour Gerda Bengtsson prefers plants with small flowers and berries. Rather than cultivated garden roses with their large, single-coloured petals, she therefore seeks out wild roses with hip berries. Most of the roses and berries are predominantly red, but yellow and white are included to contrast sensitively with the brown branches and green leaves. The browns and greens also vary subtly in shading, from light to dark, demonstrating Gerda Bengtsson's fine sense of colour.

The designs are worked in a wide range of Danish Flower Threads, but they also include light cross stitch thread and silk to provide gloss and brightness.

The author uses flowers from her own garden and those of her friends. N.G. Treschow, from the Botanical Gardens in Copenhagen, helps her by providing fresh flowers out of season and he also assists with the identification of the roses and berries.

Eric Lassen   President of The Danish Handcraft Guild

The Danish Handcraft Guild

Under the Patronage of
Her Majesty Queen Ingrid

The Danish Handcraft Guild was founded in 1928
to promote the spread of interest in needlework
and crafts in Denmark. The idea behind the
foundation was to preserve old Danish textile
traditions while supporting contemporary
innovation in the field of embroidery, knitting and
other Danish crafts.

From its design office and workshop, artists and
craftsmen create designs which are published or
produced as kits. The Guild produces a quarterly,
bilingual, (Danish/English) magazine which provides
information and news for its numerous members in
Denmark and abroad. It also publishes embroidery
books, one of the most popular of which is a
calendar of cross stitch designs contributed by
various well-known artists including Her Majesty
Queen Margrethe, the Danish Queen.

Associate membership is open to anyone
interested in the Guild.
For further information apply to:
The Danish Embroidery Centre
Little Saxham
Bury St Edmunds
Sussex

Materials and instructions

The patterns in this book are worked on 12 B linen or 10 B linen with Danish Flower Thread (Dansk Blomstergarn).

12 B linen, bleached:
Evenweave linen, 30 threads to the inch, 64 inches wide (160 cm). Danish Flower Thread: work with 1 strand using tapestry needle number 24.

10 B linen, bleached:
Evenweave linen, 27 threads to the inch. 60 inches wide (150 cm): Danish Flower Thread: work with 1 strand using tapestry needle number 22.

1 square on pattern $= 2 \times 2$ threads of linen.
NB: When working petit point: 1 square on pattern $= 1 \times 1$ thread of linen.

On all the patterns, arrows indicate the centre lines. The intersection of these lines is the centre of the pattern.

For some of the motifs Cross Stitch Thread (Amagergarn) is used: work with 1 strand. Silk: work with 1 strand, without tightening it.

The linen used in this book is a Danish evenweave called HF Linen which provides an excellent background for the cross stitch embroidery but the same effect can be obtained using a similar evenweave linen. Danish Flower Thread is a fine, mat, cotton thread available in over 100 shades (see page 9). All materials are produced by the Danish Handcraft Guild and can be obtained through the stockists listed on page 64.

Method of working

The patterns in the book are created in cross stitch. The different colours used are shown in symbols and numbers under the pattern diagrams. (In certain patterns back stitch and petit point are also used. The symbols for these are shown on the colour keys to the left of the cross stitch symbols.) The illustration on the opposite page shows the range of colours used in Danish Flower Thread with the appropriate numbers adjacent.

Cross stitch

A. Cross stitch from left to right. The underhalf of the stitch is made first, working crosswise over two threads of linen from the lower left-hand corner to the upper right-hand corner. The upper half of the stitch is made backwards as shown.

B. Cross stitch worked up and down. Each stitch is completed in one operation, so that the upper half of the stitch is in the same direction as in A. The wrong side of both A and B appears as vertical rows of stitches.

C. Cross stitches displaced in relation to each other.

D. Four $\frac{3}{4}$ cross stitches are shown on the left. On the right can be seen half cross stitches covering one thread length-wise and two threads cross-wise.

Back stitch

A. In the left-hand illustration the upper stitches are made by inserting the needle two threads to the side and two threads down, one upright stitch passes over two threads and one horizontal stitch over two threads. In the right-hand illustration the upper stitch is made two threads down but only one to the side, and one of the stitches (the fourth), is made two threads to the side and one thread down. In addition one stitch and one horizontal stitch is shown.

B. Four back stitches: two worked over a single thread and two worked on a single intersection.

Petit point

Work petit point horizontally from the right to the left, each stitch taken diagonally over one thread.

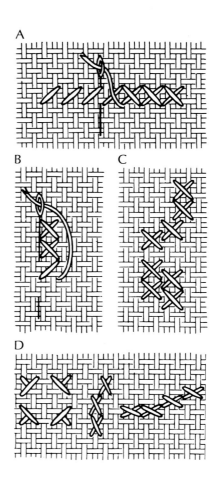

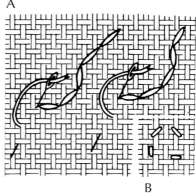

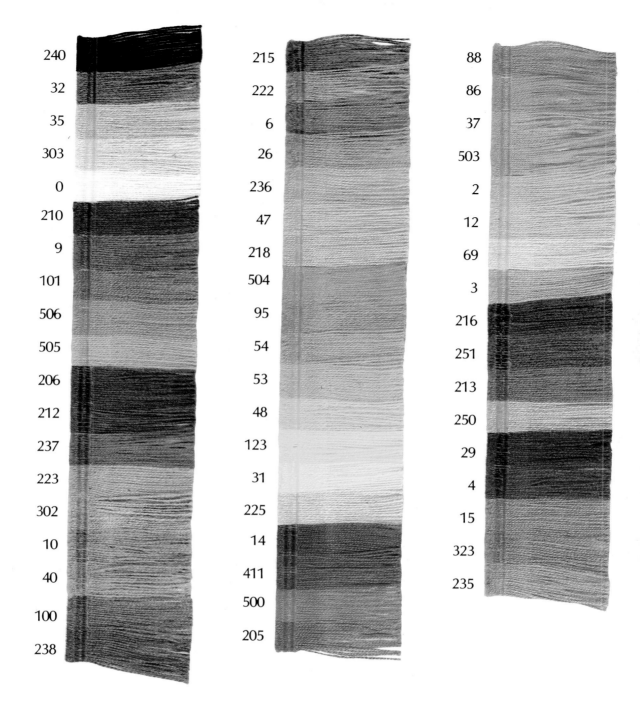

240	215	88
32	222	86
35	6	37
303	26	503
0	236	2
210	47	12
9	218	69
101	504	3
506	95	216
505	54	251
206	53	213
212	48	250
237	123	29
223	31	4
302	225	15
10	14	323
40	411	235
100	500	
238	205	

The colour key above indicates which Danish Flower Threads have been used for the embroideries in the book.

Examples of finished work

Runner
12 B linen
Cutting measurements: $12\frac{5}{8} \times 39\frac{3}{8}$in (32 × 100cm).
Finished measurements: $8 \times 35\frac{3}{8}$in (20 × 92cm).
Find centre of the shorter edge of the linen.
Measure $2\frac{3}{8}$in (6cm) up from the edge and begin the embroidery at arrow.
Distance between the two motifs about $23\frac{1}{2}$in (60cm).
Fold the linen 22 threads from the embroidery.
Sew a hem 7 threads wide, hem-stitching over 3 threads.

Wall hanging
12 B linen
Cutting measurements: $15\frac{3}{4} \times 15\frac{3}{4}$in (40 × 40cm).
Finished measurements: $10\frac{1}{2} \times 10\frac{1}{2}$in (27 × 27cm).
Find centre of the pattern with the help of the arrows.
Find the centre of the linen. Begin here.
Mount the finished embroidery on cardboard.

Cushion
10 B linen
Cutting measurements: $14\frac{1}{2} \times 29\frac{1}{2}$in (37 × 75cm).
Finished measurments: $11\frac{1}{2} \times 11\frac{1}{2}$in (29 × 29cm).
Find the centre of the pattern with the help of the arrows.
Find the centre of the linen. Begin here.
Piece cushion together with piping around edge.

Doily
12 B linen
Cutting measurements: 9 × 9in (23 × 23cm).
Finished measurements: 6 × 6in (15 × 15cm).
Find the centre of the pattern with the help of the arrows.
Find centre of the linen. Begin here.
Sew a hem 7 threads wide, hem-stitching over 3 threads.

Place mat
12 B linen
Cutting measurements: $15\frac{3}{4} \times 21$in (40 × 53cm).
Finished measurements: $11\frac{3}{4} \times 16$in (30 × 41cm).
Measure $2\frac{1}{4}$in (6cm) in and down from the top lefthand corner. Begin the border here. Fold under the linen 7 threads from the embroidery and sew a hem 7 threads wide.

In addition to the suggestions on the opposite page the photograph shows how you can apply your designs to a variety of pretty articles.

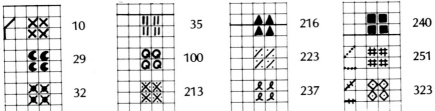

	10		35		216		240
	29		100		223		251
	32		213		237		323

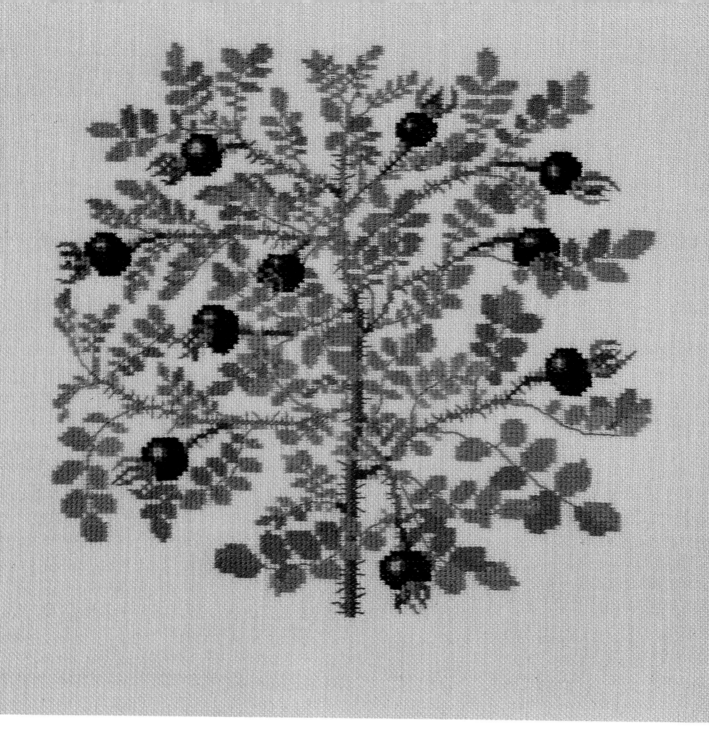

ROSA PIMPINELLIFOLIA

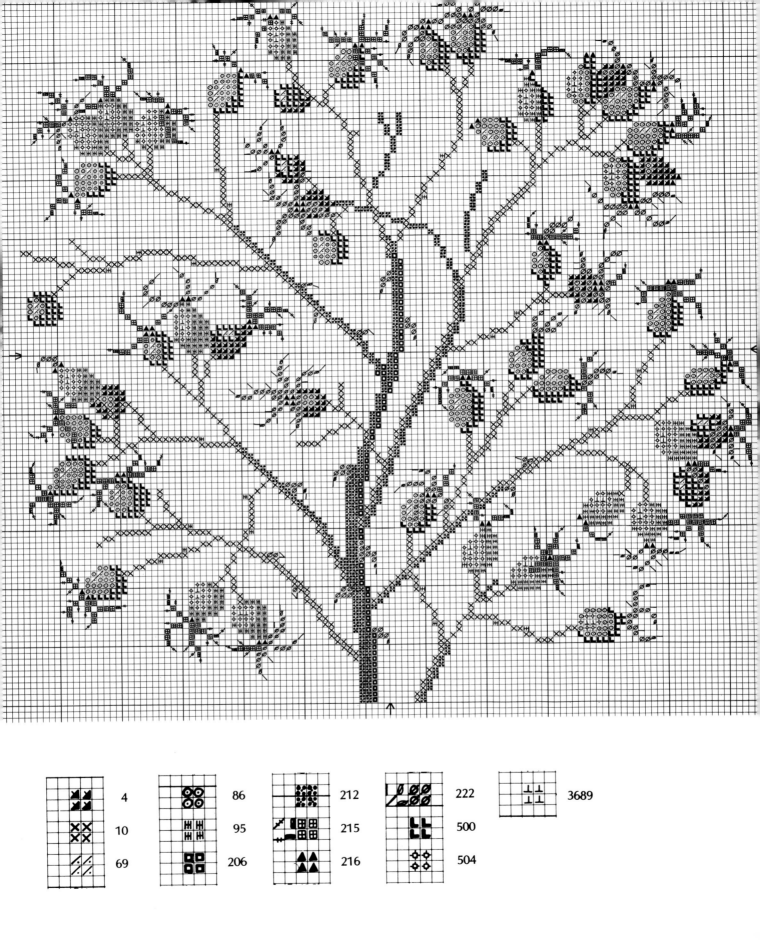

Eglantine — Sweet Briar

ROSA RUBIGINOSA

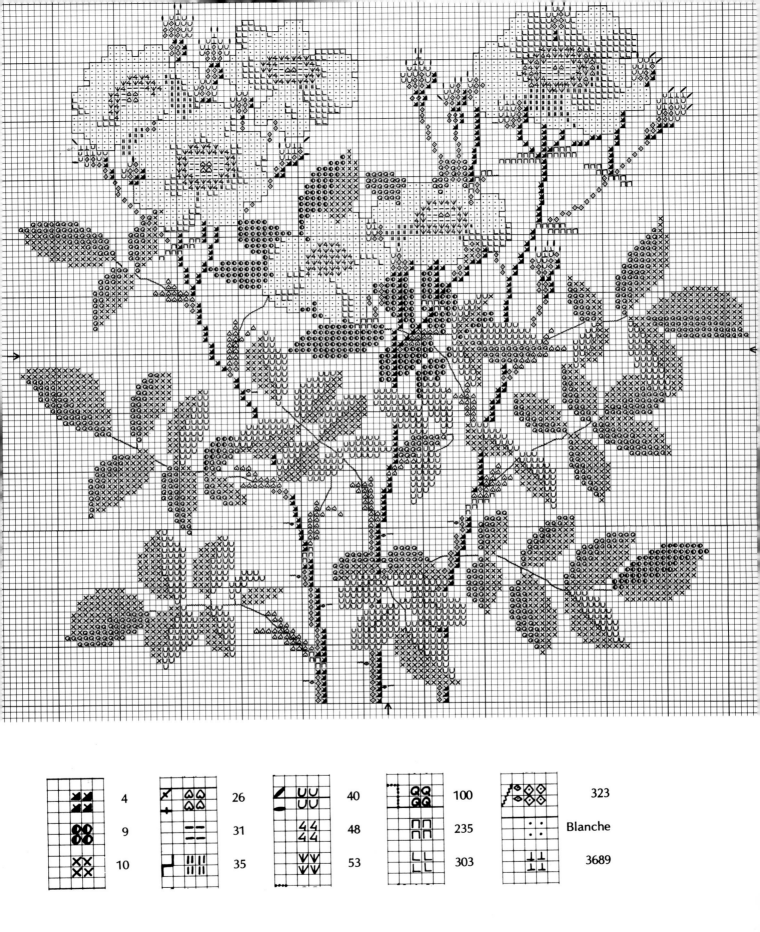

	4		26		40		100	323
	9		31		48		235	Blanche
	10		35		53		303	3689

Field Rose

ROSA ARVENSIS

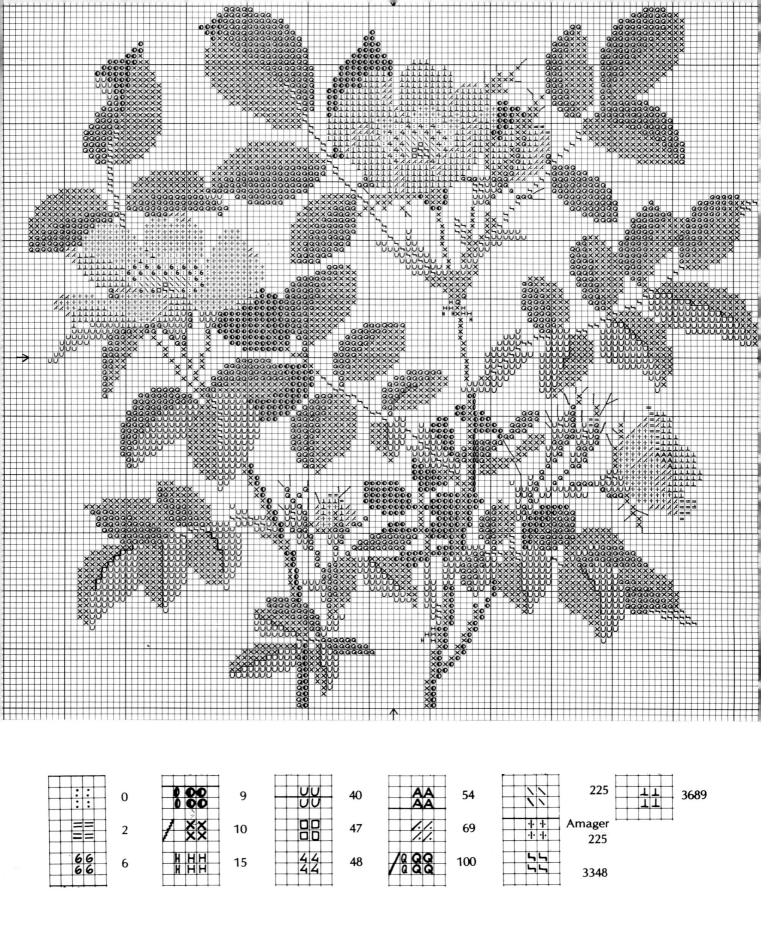

0	9	40	54	225
2	10	47	69	Amager 225
6	15	48	100	3348

3689

Dog Rose

ROSA CANINA

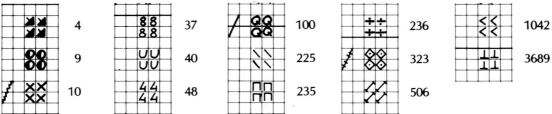

◢◣	4	8 8	37	/ ◖◗	100	+ +	236	< <	1042
◖◗	9	U U	40	\ \	225	◈ ◈	323	⊥ ⊥	3689
X X	10	4 4	48	⊓ ⊓	235	◸◹	506		

ROSA VIRGINIANA

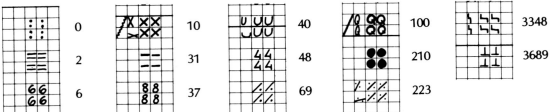

	0		10		40		100		3348
	2		31		48		210		3689
	6		37		69		223		

Eglantine – Sweet Briar

ROSA RUBIGINOSA

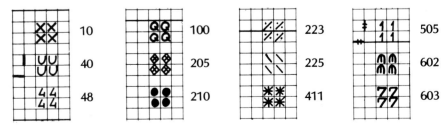

XX	10	
UU	40	
44	48	
QQ	100	
⊗⊗	205	
●●	210	
⁄⁄	223	
＼＼	225	
✳✳	411	
11	505	
ɯɯ	602	
ƵƵ	603	

ROSA RUGOSA

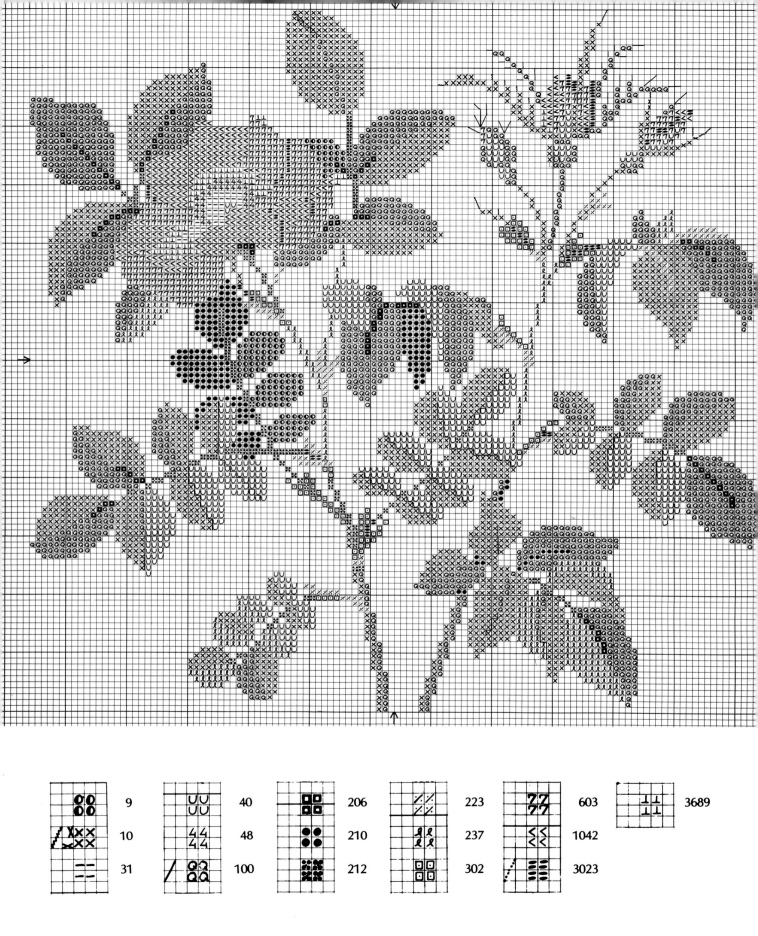

○○ / ○○	9	U U / U U	40	■□ / □■	206	╱╱ / ╱╱	223
╱Xx╱ / Xxx╱	10	4 4 / 4 4	48	●● / ●●	210	⅄⅄ / ⅄⅄	237
─ ─ / ─ ─	31	╱ QQ / QQ	100	❖❖ / ❖❖	212	□□ / □□	302

77 / 77	603	⊥⊥ / ⊥⊥	3689
<< / <<	1042		
⋮ ❱❱ / ❱❱	3023		

French Rose

ROSA GALLICA

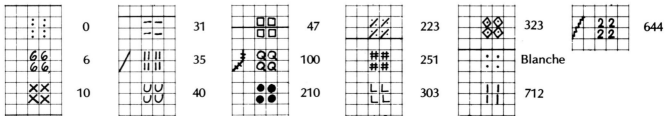

	0		31		47		223		323		644
	6		35		100		251		Blanche		712
	10		40		210		303				

'Nevada'

ROSA MOYESII

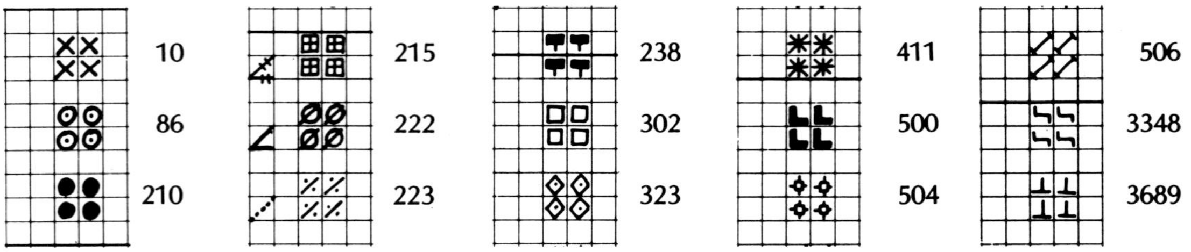

✕✕ / ✕✕	10	⊞⊞ / ⊞⊞	215	⊤⊤ / ⊤⊤	238	✳✳ / ✳✳	411	⊘⊘	506
⊙⊙ / ⊙⊙	86	⊘⊘ / ⊘⊘	222	□□ / □□	302	ᴸᴸ / ᴸᴸ	500	�5�5	3348
●● / ●●	210	⁄⁄ / ⁄⁄	223	◇◇ / ◇◇	323	◇◇ / ◇◇	504	⊥⊥ / ⊤⊤	3689

'Frau Dagmar Hartopp'

ROSA RUGOSA

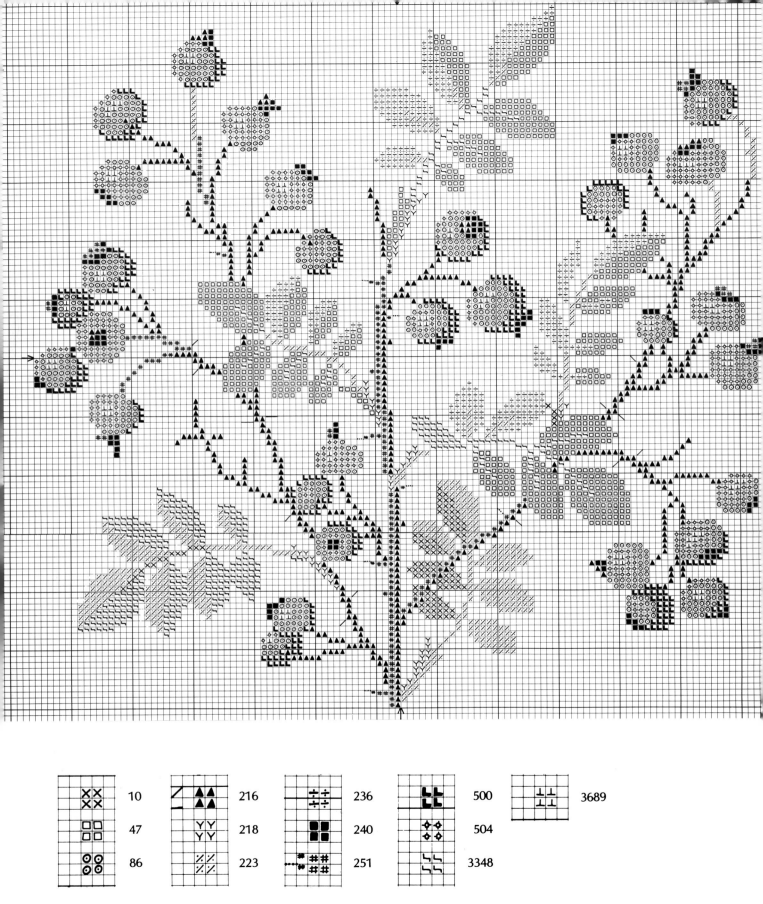

XX / XX	10	
□□ / □□	47	
⊙⊙ / ⊙⊙	86	

▲▲ / ▲▲	216	
YY / YY	218	
⁄. ⁄.	223	

÷ ÷	236	
■■ / ■■	240	
# #	251	

LL / LL	500	
◆◆	504	
⌐⌐	3348	

⊥⊥ / ⊥⊥	3689

ROSA NITIDA

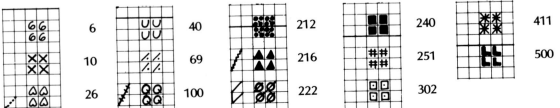

6 6 / 6 6		6
X X / X X		10
△ △ / △ △		26

U U / U U		40
/ / / /		69
Q Q / Q Q		100

● ● / ● ●		212
▲ ▲ / ▲ ▲		216
Ø Ø / Ø Ø		222

■ ■ / ■ ■		240
# # / # #		251
▯ ▯ / ▯ ▯		302

✳ ✳ / ✳ ✳		411
L L / L L		500

ROSA SERAFINE

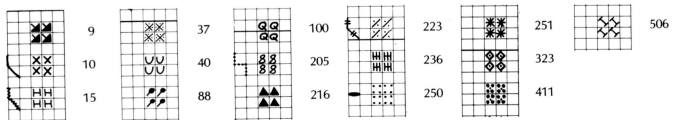

9
10
15

37
40
88

100
205
216

223
236
250

251
323
411

506

ROSA MOYESII

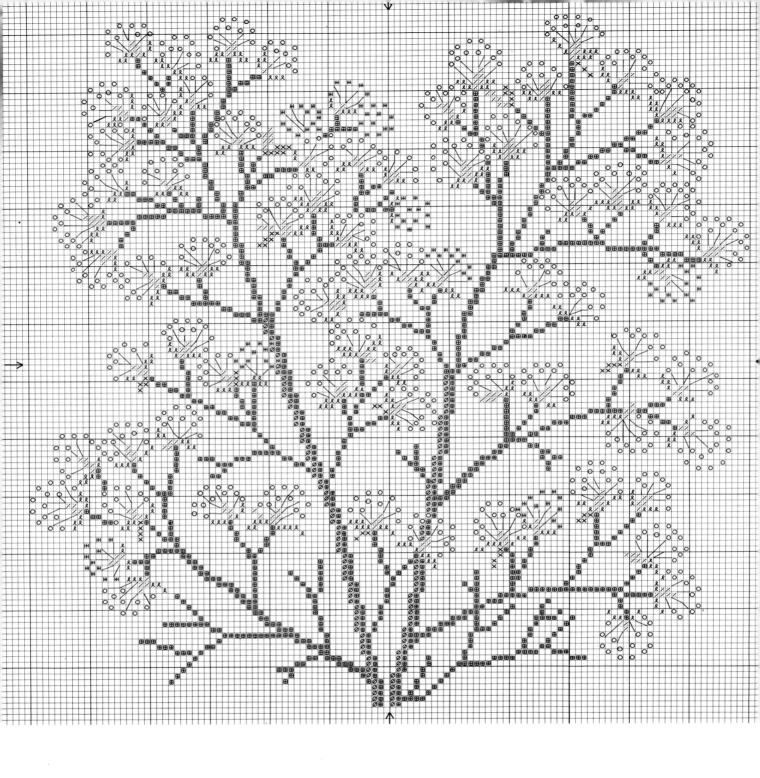

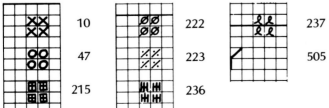

✕✕	10
○○	47
⊞⊞	215

∅∅	222
⁄⁄	223
⾙⾙	236

ℓℓ	237
╱	505

Cornelian Cherry

CORNUS MAS

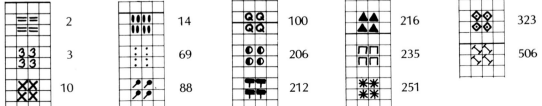

	2		14		100		216		323
	3		69		206		235		506
	10		88		212		251		

Ornamental Almond

PRUNUS PERSICA

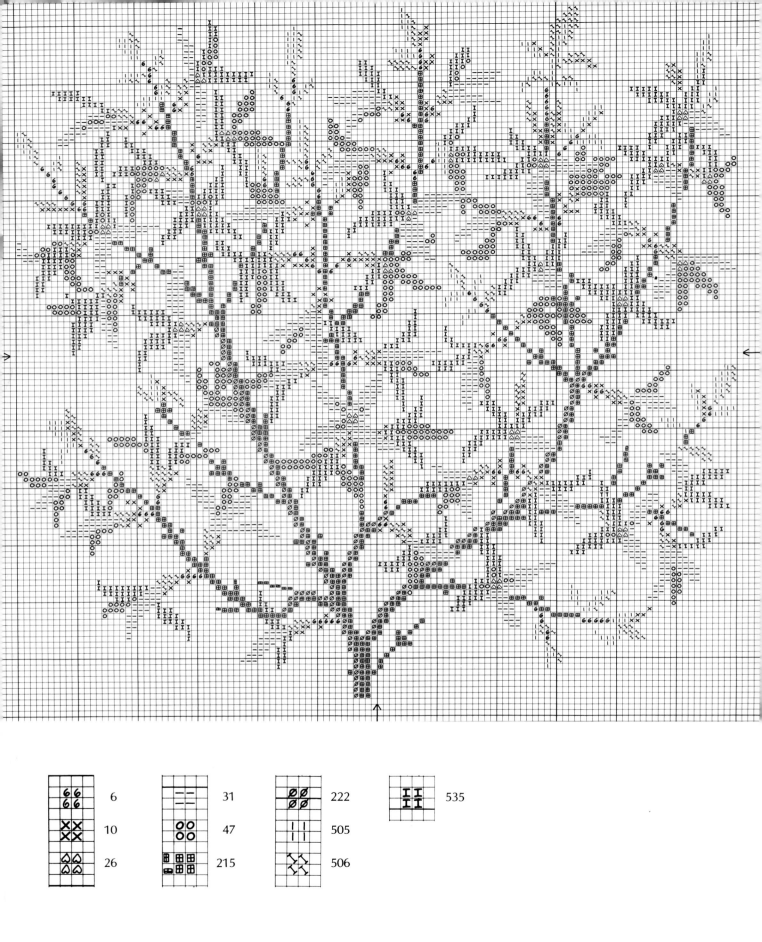

6 6 / 6 6	6	
X X / X X	10	
△ △ / △ △	26	

− − / − −	31	
○ ○ / ○ ○	47	
⊞ ⊞ / ⊞ ⊞	215	

∅ ∅ / ∅ ∅	222	
I I / I I	505	
↖ ↗ / ↙ ↘	506	

I I / I I	535

Forsythia

FORSYTHIA INTERMEDIA

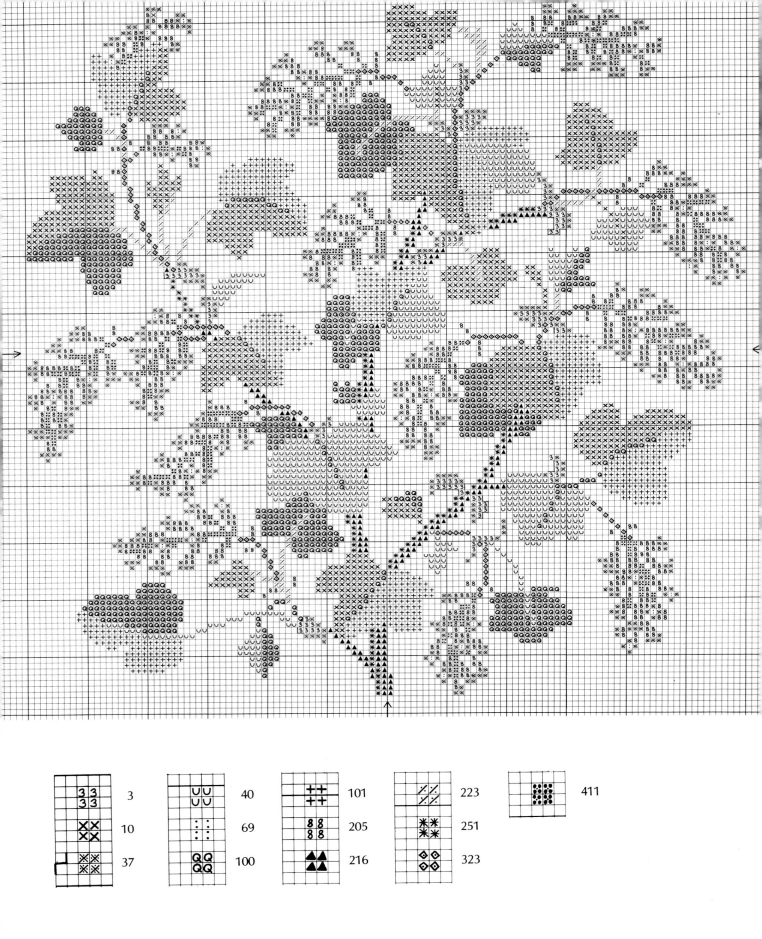

	3		40		101		223		411
	10		69		205		251		
	37		100		216		323		

Flowering Currant

RIBES SANGUINEUM

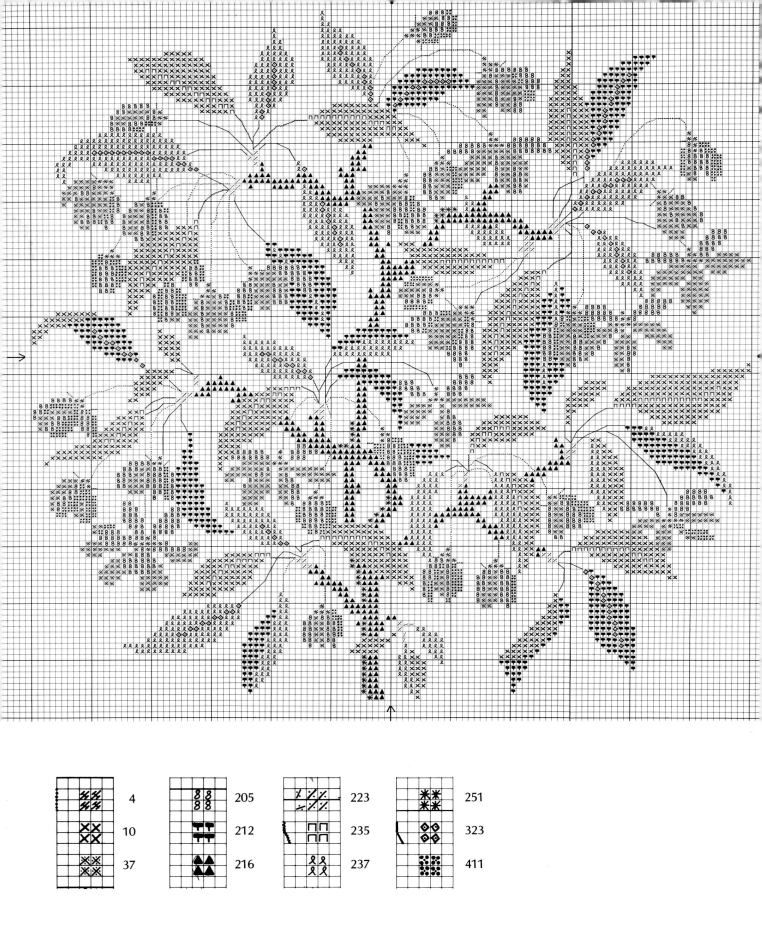

	4		205		223		251
	10		212		235		323
	37		216		237		411

Crab Apple

MALUS PURPUREA

6 6 / 6 6	6		
X X / X X	10		
X X / X X	37		

Q Q / Q Q	100
8 8 / 8 8	205
▲ ▲ / ▲ ▲	216

Y Y / Y Y	218
∕ ∕ / ∕ ∕	223
∴∴ / ∴∴	225

✳✳ / ✳✳	251
l l / l l	505
⋋⋋ / ⋋⋋	506

L L / L L	3012

RHODODENDRON HIRSUTUM

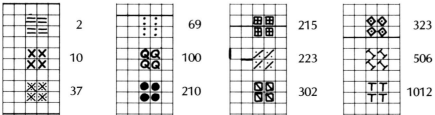

	2		69		215		323
	10		100		223		506
	37		210		302		1012

WEIGELA FLORIDA

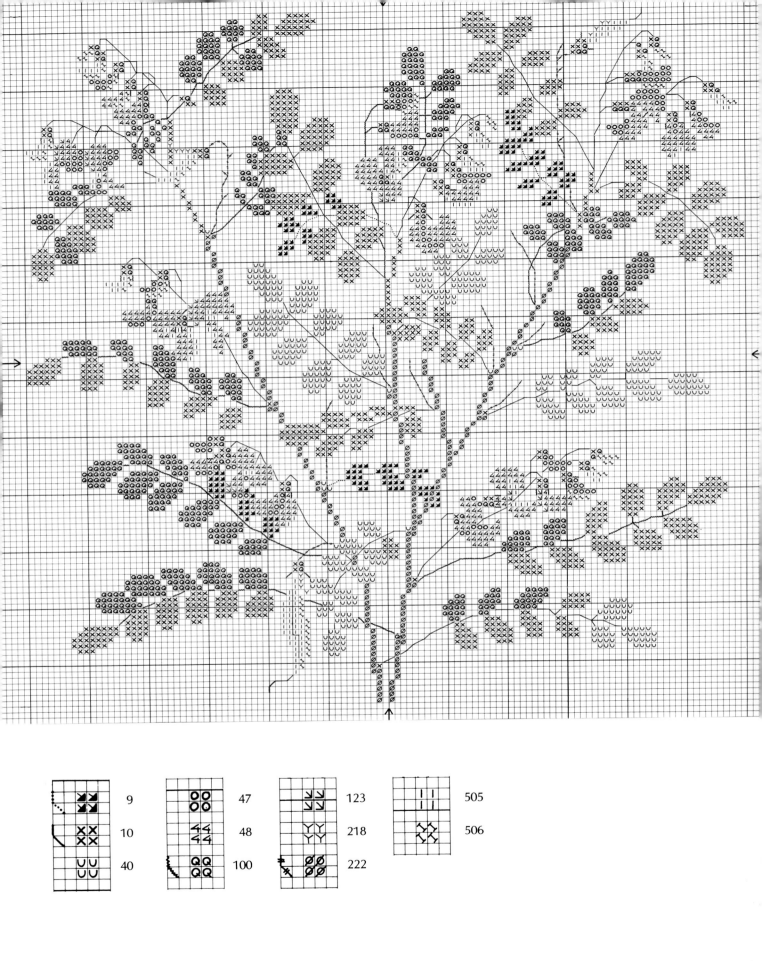

9	47	123	505
10	48	218	506
40	100	222	

Senna

COLUTEA ARBORESCENS

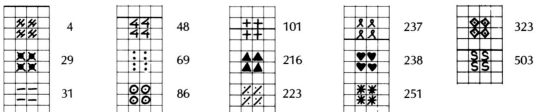

	4		48		101		237		323
	29		69		216		238		503
	31		86		223		251		

Japanese Quince

CHAENOMELES LAGENARIA

55

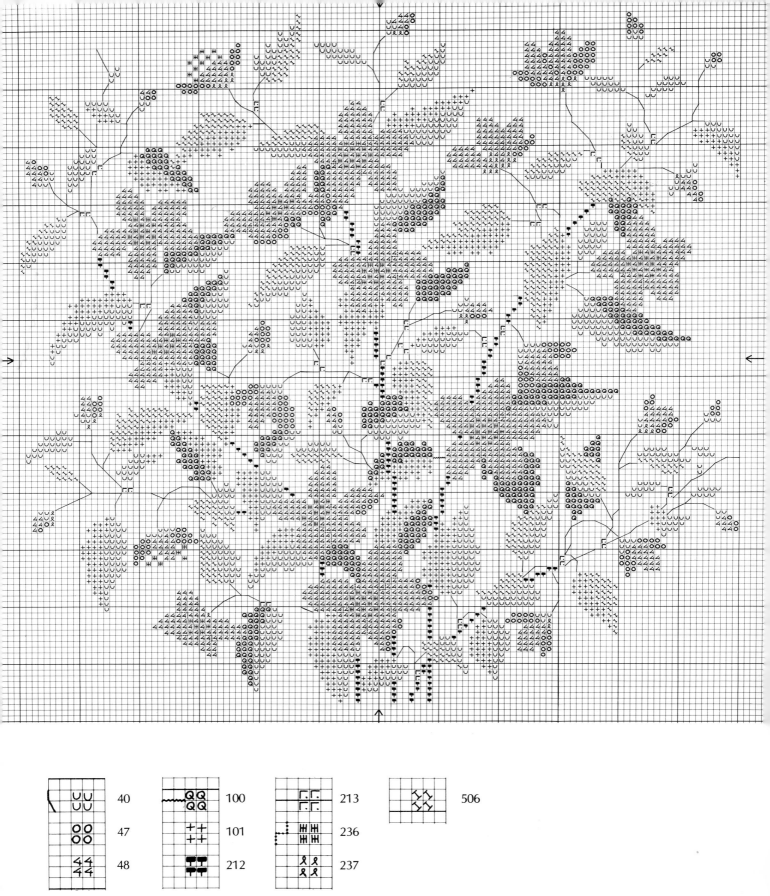

∪∪ / ∪∪	40	~~QQ / QQ	100
OO / OO	47	++ / ++	101
44 / 44	48	▜▜ / ▜▜	212

Γ.Γ. / Γ.Γ.	213
ⱧⱧ / ⱧⱧ	236
ⱷⱷ / ⱷⱷ	237

⅄⅄ / ⅄⅄	506

KERRIA JAPONICA

XX / XX	10	++ / +	101
UU / UU	40	●● / ●●	210
QQ / QQ	100	⊞⊞ / ⊞⊞	215

⊓⊓ / ⊓⊓	235	QQ / QQ	1042
⊠⊠ / ⊠⊠	302	☰☰ / ☰☰	3023
◇◇ / ◇◇	323		

INDIGOFERA GERARDIANA

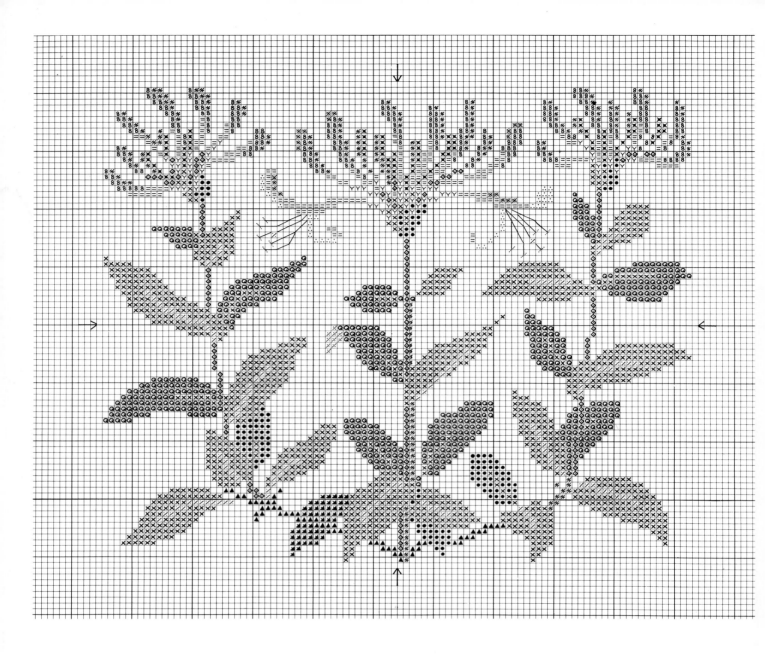

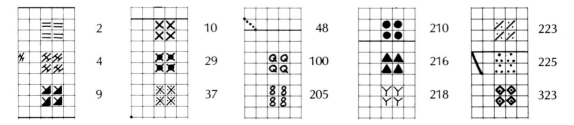

	2		10		48		210		223
	4		29		100		216		225
	9		37		205		218		323

Honeysuckle

LONICERA PERICLYMENUM

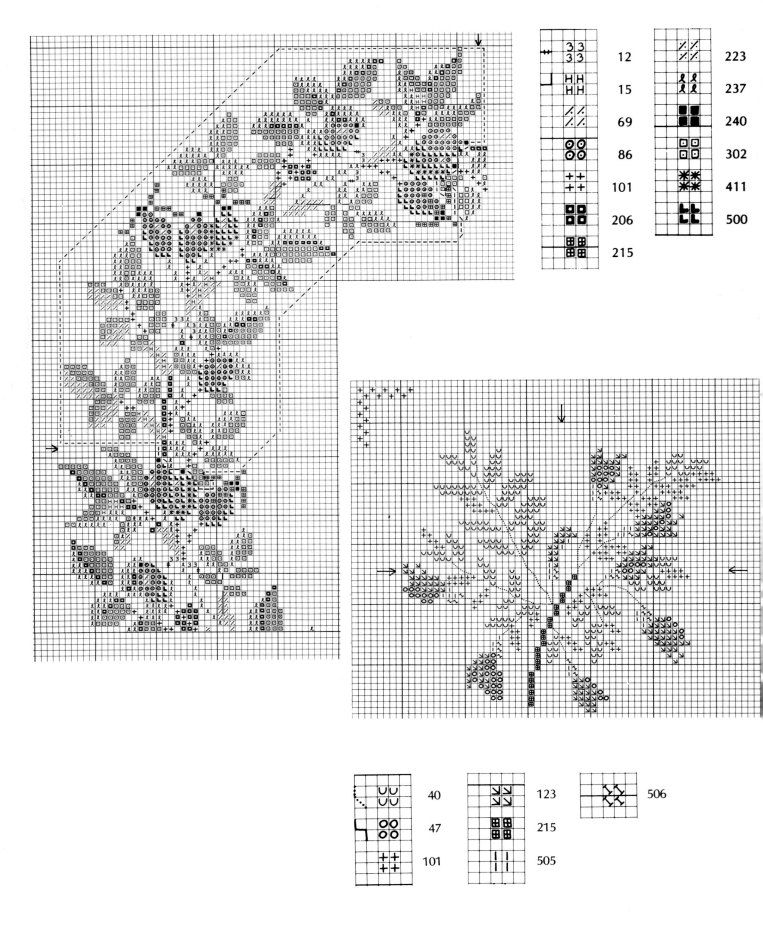

⊢⊣ 3 3 / 3 3	12	⁄ ⁄ / ⁄ ⁄
⌐ H H / H H	15	ʃ ʃ / ʃ ʃ
⁄ ⁄ / ⁄ ⁄	69	■ ■ / ■ ■
○○ / ○○	86	▫□ / ▫□
+ + / + +	101	❋ ❋ / ❋ ❋
◨□ / ◨□	206	L L / L L
⊞⊞ / ⊞⊞	215	

		223
		237
		240
		302
		411
		500

∪∪ / ∪∪	40	⋎⋎ / ⋎⋎	123
○○ / ○○	47	⊞⊞ / ⊞⊞	215
+ + / + +	101	ǀ ǀ / ǀ ǀ	505

⋈ ⋈ / ⋈ ⋈	506

Dog Rose

ROSA CANINA

CARAGANA FRUCTICOSA

List of patterns

Suppliers in Great Britain

Details of other stockists of Danish Handcraft Guild supplies can be obtained by sending an s.a.e. to the main distributors: The Silver Thimble, The Old Malthouse, Clarence Street, Bath, Avon BA1 5NS. Danish Flower Threads and linens can be obtained from the following:

Artisan
22 High Street
Pinner
Middlesex

Campden Needlecraft Centre
High Street
Chipping Campden
Gloucestershire

S N Cooke
18 Wood Street
Stratford on Avon
Warwick

Danish Embroidery Centre
Little Saxham
Bury St Edmunds
Sussex

The Gentle Art
29 Seaside Road
Eastbourne
Sussex

Helens
55–57 Teme Street
Tenbury Wells
Worcestershire

Lalla Thomas Ltd
413/415 Abergele Road
Old Colwyn
Colwyn Bay
Clwyd

Liberty & Co Ltd
Regent Street
London W1

Leven Crafts
The Minstrels Gallery
21 Chaloner Street
Guisborough
Cleveland

Mace & Nairn
89 Crane Street
Salisbury
Wiltshire

Needle Needs Ltd
20 Beauchamp Place
London SW3

The Needlewoman
21 Needless Alley
Birmingham

The Nimble Thimble
26 The Green
Bolton
Rugby

Richmond Arts & Crafts
181 City Road
Cardiff

Christine Riley
53 Barclay Street
Stonehaven
Kincardineshire

Royal School of Needlework
25 Princess Gate
London SW7

Russells
30 Castle Street
Carlisle
Cumbria

The Silver Thimble
33 Gay Street
Bath
Avon

Spinning Jenny
Bradley
Keighley
West Yorkshire

Teazle Embroideries
35 Boothferry Road
Hull
North Humberside